Owl

Written by Barrie Wade
Photographed by Tony Phelps
Illustrated by Andrew Midgley

Collins Educational

In a barn
in the dark
the owl waits.

In a barn
in the dark
a chick chips its way
out of an egg.

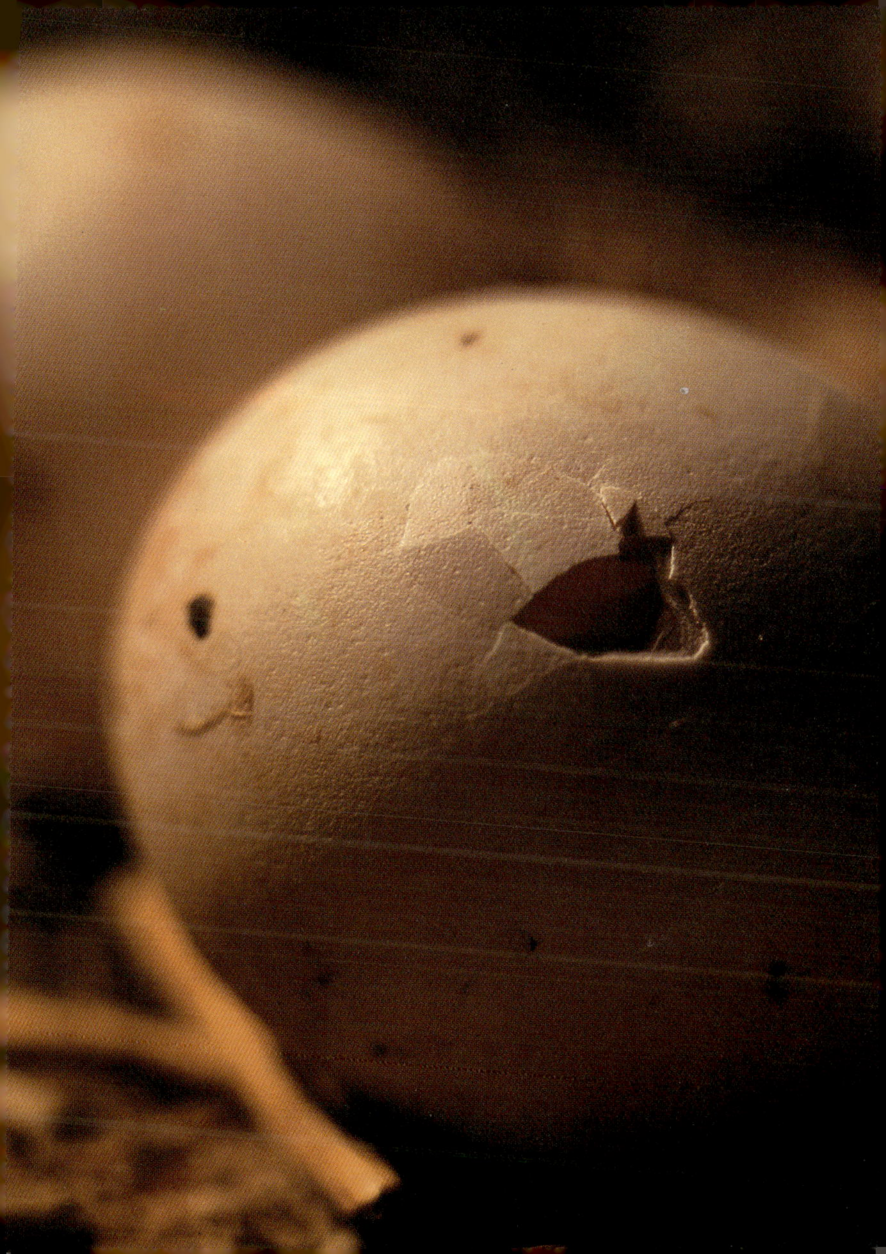

In the dusty barn
in the dark night
the chick lies resting.

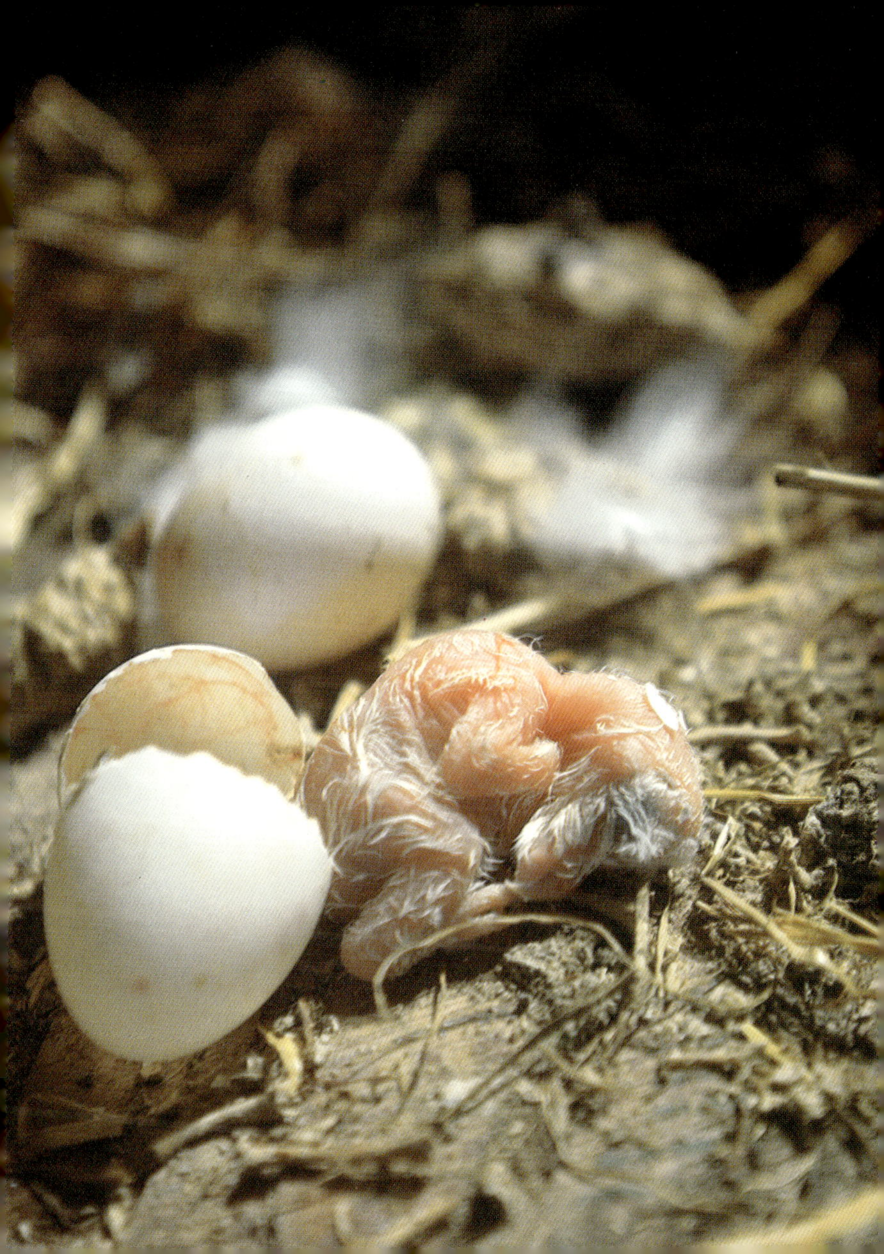

In the dusty barn
dark nights pass by
and the chick
grows feathers.

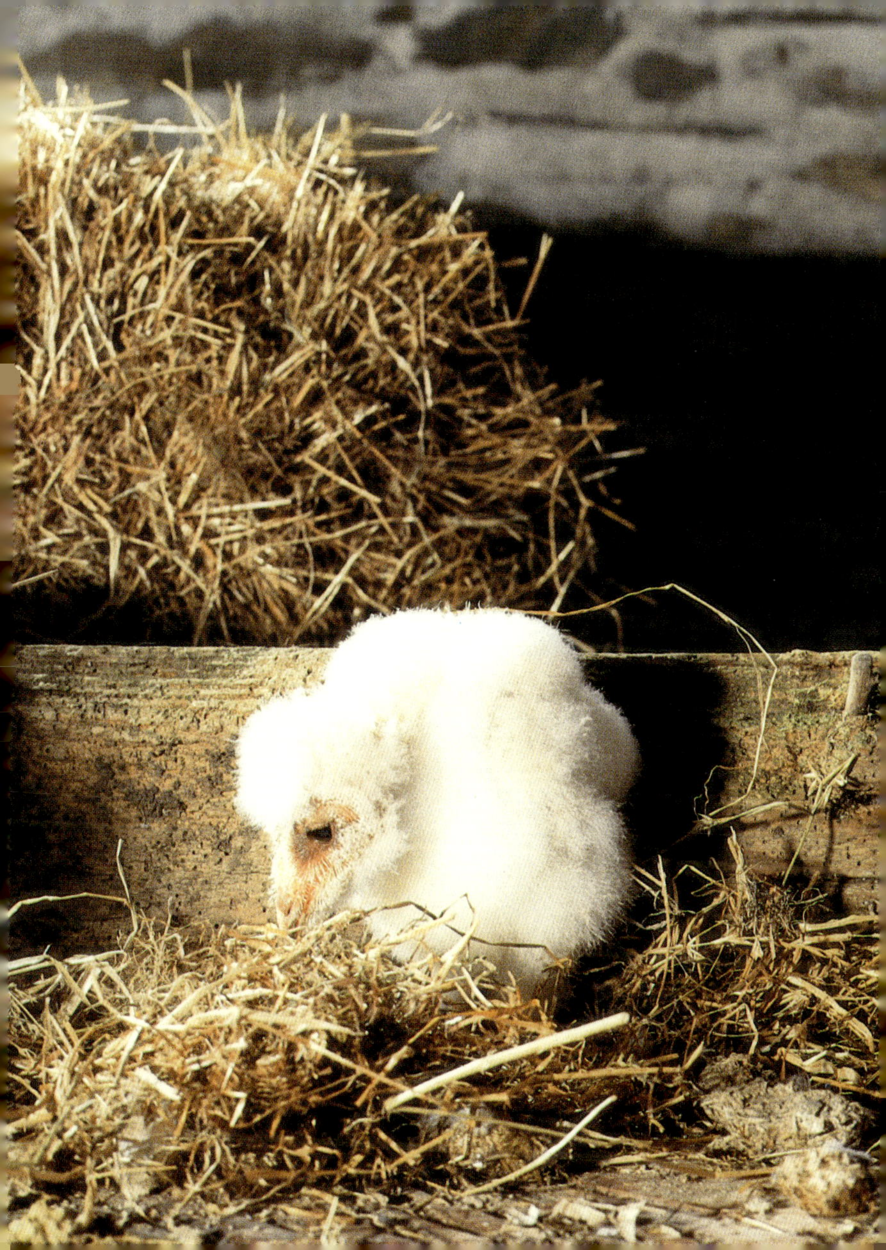

In the dark, dusty barn
night after night
the owl watches
as the chick grows.

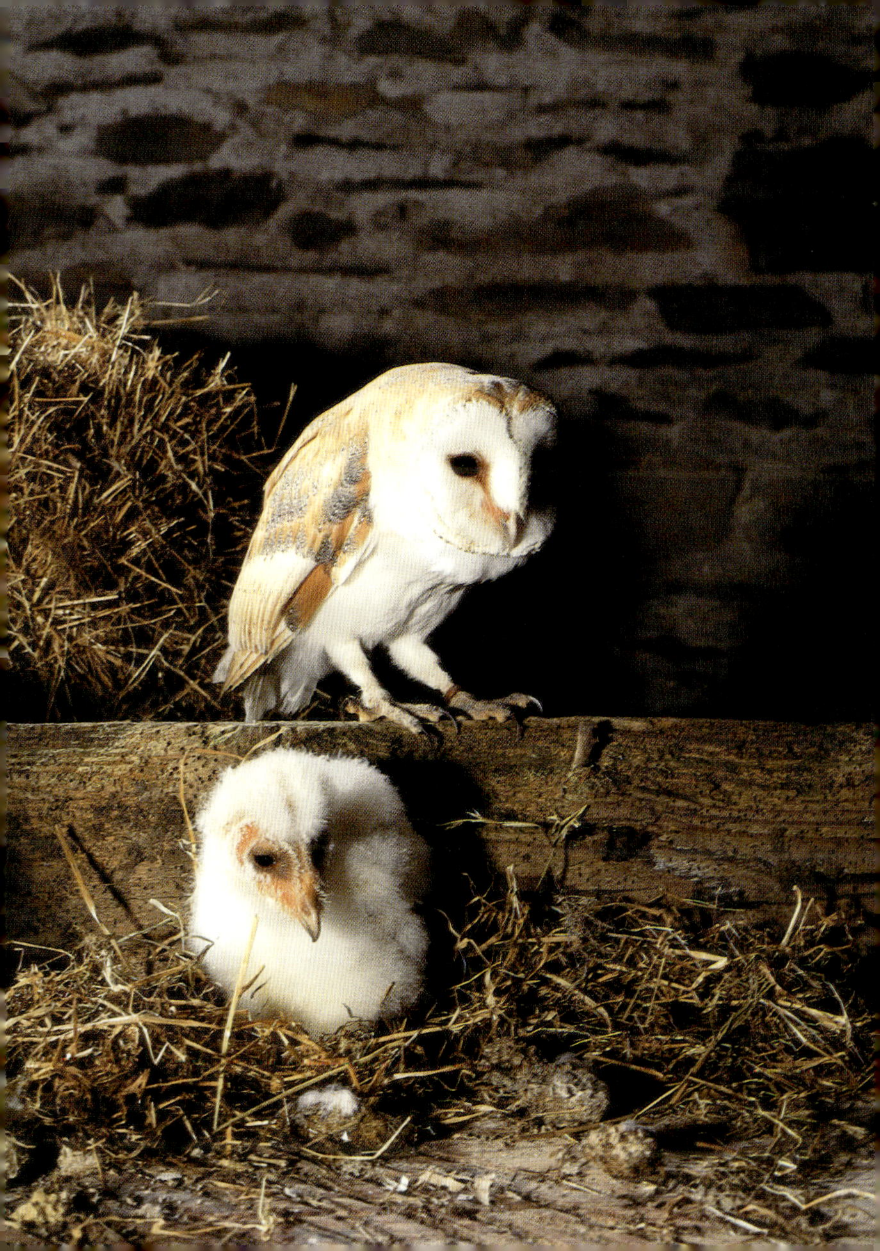

In the dark, dusty barn
in the deep dark night
the young owl grows…

a strong beak to bite,

sharp claws to clutch,

a face like a dish.

Out of the dark,
dusty barn
into the dusk
the young owl flies.